D1265884

AVAILABLE NOW
from Lerner Publishing Services!

The *On the Hardwood* series:

Atlanta Hawks	Los Angeles Lakers
Boston Celtics	Memphis Grizzlies
Brooklyn Nets	Miami Heat
Chicago Bulls	Minnesota Timberwolves
Cleveland Cavaliers	New York Knicks
Dallas Mavericks	Oklahoma City Thunder
Denver Nuggets	Phoenix Suns
Detroit Pistons	Philadelphia 76ers
Golden State Warriors	Portland Trail Blazers
Houston Rockets	San Antonio Spurs
Indiana Pacers	Utah Jazz
Los Angeles Clippers	Washington Wizards

Hoop City   Long Shot

Basketball fans: *don't miss these hoops books from MVP's wing-man, Scobre Educational.*

These titles, and many others, are available at www.scobre.com.

ON THE HARDWOOD

MEMPHIS GRIZZLIES

J.M. SKOGEN

On the Hardwood: Memphis Grizzlies

MVP Books
2255 Calle Clara
La Jolla, CA 92037

MVP Books is an imprint of Scobre Educational, a division of Book Buddy Digital Media, Inc.,
42982 Osgood Road, Fremont, CA 94539

MVP Books publications may be purchased for
educational, business, or sales promotional use.

Cover and layout design by Jana Ramsay
Copy edited by Susan Sylvia
Photos by Getty Images

ISBN: 978-1-61570-918-2 (Library Binding)
ISBN: 978-1-61570-917-5 (Soft Cover)

TABLE OF CONTENTS

In the spring of 2013, the Memphis Grizzlies—one of Tennessee's only professional sports teams—were on fire. These underdogs, who had never advanced past the Western Conference Semifinals, were preparing to take on some of the best teams in the league during the playoffs. As sportscasters wondered if the little team from Tennessee had finally found its teeth, Grizzlies fans were riding high. Would this finally be the year of the Grizzlies? The year they reached the Western Conference Finals? Or even, some fans dared to hope, became

Tigers and Bears...Oh My!
The University of Memphis Tigers also play in FedExForum.

NBA Champions?

Grizzlies fans had good reason to hope for a spectacular playoff run. Memphis had roared into the

The Memphis Grizzlies dominated during the 2012-13 regular season.

7

playoffs with a franchise-best 56-26 regular season record. Early in the 2012-13 season, fans received a taste of how big the year would potentially be. Though the Grizzlies lost their first game of the season, they won the next eight. The only team with a better record during the first few weeks of the 2012-13 season was the New York Knicks—until the Grizzlies ended New York's perfect 6-0 record with a 105-95 victory on November 16th. Memphis went on to win 32 out of their 41 home games during the regular season, proving that the Grizzlies were nearly impossible to beat on their home court.

Simply put, the 2012-13 season was the best that Memphis had ever seen. Center Marc Gasol was turning heads across the country. After his spectacular regular season performance, Gasol won the NBA Defensive Player

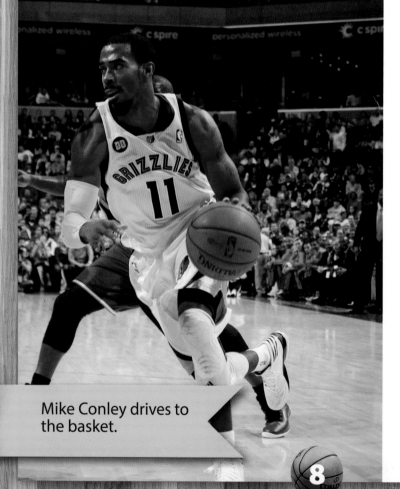

Mike Conley drives to the basket.

of the Year award—making him the first Grizzly to ever claim that honor. Other players, like veteran forward Zach Randolph, young guard Mike Conley, and the team's "spiritual leader" Tony Allen, filled out the roster with strong, dependable talent.

During the first round of the playoffs, fans crowded into FedExForum in Memphis, Tennessee, eager to watch their team take on the Los Angeles Clippers. The Clippers ousted the Grizzlies from the opening round of the playoffs the previous season, so Memphis not only wanted a victory, they also craved redemption.

Marc Gasol scores against the L.A. Clippers during the 2013 Western Conference playoffs.

Only, when Memphis Grizzlies fans flooded the arena, they didn't call it FedExForum. It became the "Grindhouse." NBA blogger Jeff Caplan shed light on FedExForum's

At the Movies
In 2007, Quentin Tarantino directed an action / horror double-feature movie called *Grindhouse*.

strange nickname: "The Memphis Grizzlies' home gym didn't derive its horror-flick nickname from the deafening screams of a zealous fandom. The 'Grindhouse' was born from the team's sweat-and-blood, grit-&-grind style, and bequeathed by Memphis guard Tony Allen, the ultimate grit-&-grind Grizz."

Caplan's quote refers to a comment Tony Allen—the Grizzlies tough swingman—had made after a hard-fought victory against the OKC Thunder in 2011: "All heart. Grit. Grind." These words became a kind of team motto: a never-give-up ideal that fans could root for, and players could aspire to. By the 2012-13 season, the "Grindhouse" had become the place where other teams came to be ground into the hardwood by the Grizzlies' unmatched

Grizzlies fans turn FedExForum into the "Grindhouse."

defense, and determined offense. This "grit-&-grind" mentality applied, not just to the Grizzlies as a basketball team, but also to the hard-working people of Memphis. Tony Allen also said: "The city is something similar. Nothing was really given to the city. People are always overlooking the city too…I think people understand our struggles. They know everything wasn't peaches and cream starting out. But we made our way, and we were able to overcome a lot of things."

The first round of the playoffs didn't start well for the Grizzlies. They played the first two games in

Zach Randoph shoots in between the Clippers' Lamar Odom and Chris Paul.

Tony Allen celebrates the Grizzlies' first round playoff victory in 2013.

L.A., and, much to Memphis' dismay, the Clippers won both of them. But Grizzlies fans weren't worried. They knew they just needed to get the Clippers on their home court, and let the "Grindhouse" take care of them.

The Grindfather

Tony Allen is nicknamed "The Grindfather"—a play on the *The Godfather* movies—because he invented the Grizzlies' "Grit-&-Grind" motto.

Sure enough, with Memphis fans cheering them on, the Grizzlies won the next four games—three at home, and one back in L.A. After grinding the Clippers to an early playoffs exit, the Grizzlies would next face the Thunder. The young team from Oklahoma City, which had advanced all the way to the NBA Finals in 2012, would not be easy to beat. Some critics were convinced that Memphis would just be a short stopover for OKC, and their star Kevin Durant, on their way to the Western Conference Finals.

Even if the Grizzlies went no further than the Western Conference Semifinals, 2012-13 would have been a great season for Memphis. They had only advanced to the Conference Semifinals once in their 17-year franchise history. In 2010-11, they had also faced the Thunder in the Conference Semifinals. After a long seven-game series, the Grizzlies' title hopes were erased by the young team from OKC. For players like Marc

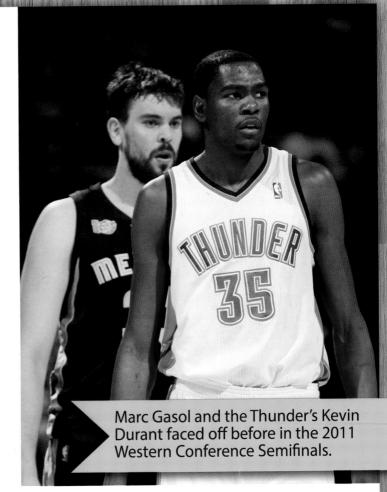

Marc Gasol and the Thunder's Kevin Durant faced off before in the 2011 Western Conference Semifinals.

Gasol, who had experienced both the joy of victory, and that bitter Game 7 loss back in 2011, the 2013 playoffs were a chance to prove how far the Grizzlies had come in just a few short years.

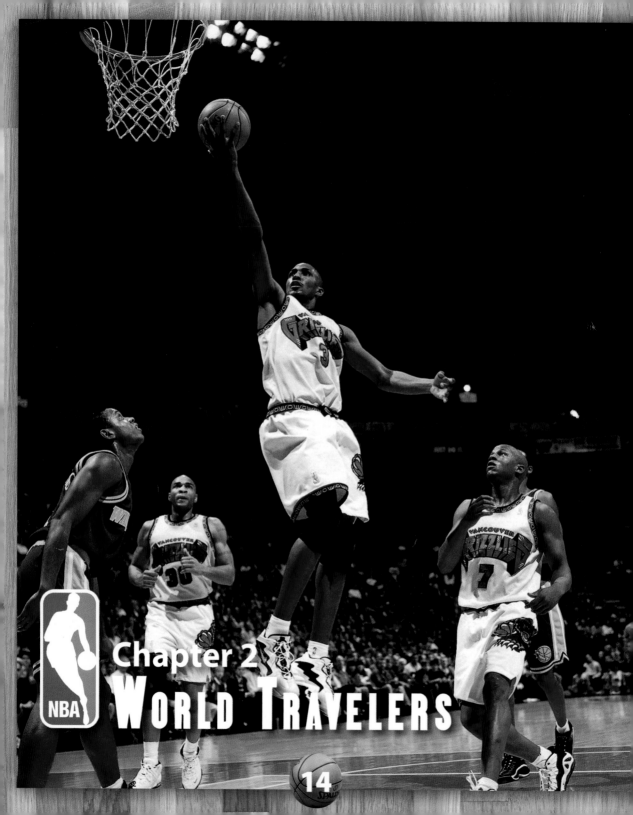

Chapter 2
WORLD TRAVELERS

14

If you venture into the Tennessee wilderness, you should be careful—you might just come across a bear. In the Great Smokey Mountains National Park, along the southern border of Tennessee, there are estimated to be about 1,500 black bears. Black bears are exciting to see in the wild, but they can be very dangerous, especially mother bears protecting their young.

Luckily for hikers in Tennessee, a black bear is nothing like a grizzly bear. A grizzly is usually lighter in color, and can be up to two times larger than a black bear. Grizzlies are also much more aggressive. It is possible to scare a black bear away by shouting, and waving your arms to make yourself look bigger. But don't try that with a grizzly. If you are actually attacked by a grizzly bear, some experts recommend covering your head and neck with your arms, and playing dead. If a grizzly thinks that you are a threat, it will not back down. But don't worry. If you visit Memphis, you are much more likely to meet a

It is very dangerous to approach a grizzly bear, especially a mother with a cub.

Grizz, the Memphis Grizzlies' mascot, gets the crowd pumped up before Game 6 of the Western Conference first round.

Grizzly on a basketball court than in the woods. There are no wild grizzly bears in Tennessee.

But then...how did the Memphis Grizzlies get their name? Why aren't they the Memphis Black Bears? To find the answer, you

Award-Winning Bear

Grizz often volunteers in schools and local hospitals. In 2011, he was voted Mascot of the Year.

should think of an entirely different part of the world. A whole different country, actually. Picture rugged mountains and tall evergreens. Clear streams silver with salmon. The Memphis Grizzlies were originally the Vancouver Grizzlies. Vancouver is a city on the West coast of British Columbia, Canada, just north of Washington State. Grizzly bears are one of British Columbia's fiercest and most majestic native animals.

Before 1995, every single NBA team was located in the United States. The Vancouver Grizzlies, along with the Toronto Raptors, made history as the first two Canadian NBA expansion teams when they joined the league for the 1995-96 season. It was very appropriate that the NBA had finally spread north to Canada—after all, James Naismith, the inventor of basketball, was born in Canada.

During the Vancouver Grizzlies' six years in the NBA, they had a few outstanding players. Shareef Abdur-Rahim, for example, was a

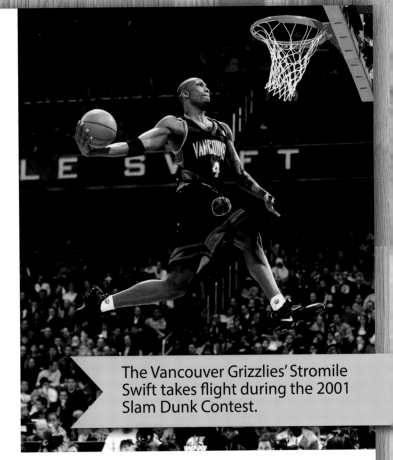

The Vancouver Grizzlies' Stromile Swift takes flight during the 2001 Slam Dunk Contest.

versatile forward who led the team in scoring. He brought attention to Vancouver when he was selected for the 1996 All-Rookie First Team, and came very close to snagging the 1996 NBA Rookie of the Year award (he finished third). Shareef, who had been nicknamed "Mr. Basketball"

Shareef Abdur-Rahim: Mr. Basketball.

attendance had dropped pretty low in Vancouver after a few seasons, and the franchise was losing a lot of money. Also, draft selections for new expansion teams were more limited, and some free-agents simply did not want to move to a different country to play basketball. In 2001, new owner Michael Heisley made it clear that the Grizzlies would not continue to play in Vancouver. But where would the team go?

Moving an NBA franchise from one city to another was not unheard of, but it was not common. As of 2001, the last NBA team to change cities was the Kings, when they

while at college, became the face of Vancouver's young franchise.

Even with a star on their team, the Vancouver Grizzlies never had a winning season. Most expansion teams take a number of years to find the right mix of players, and coaching staff, before they really become competitive. Unfortunately, moved from Kansas City, Missouri, to Sacramento, California, in 1985. The NBA would not relocate a team without a good reason, and without solid groundwork being laid first. If Heisley wanted to move the Grizzlies, he would have to find them a new home that could support a growing franchise.

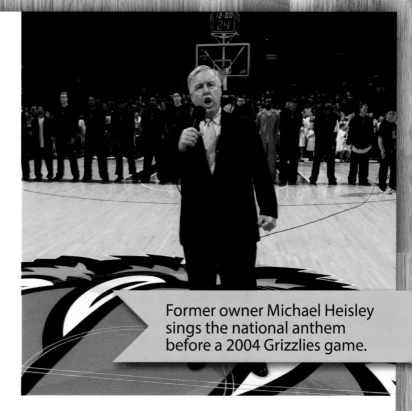

Former owner Michael Heisley sings the national anthem before a 2004 Grizzlies game.

Enter Memphis, Tennessee. Memphis, a city known across the country for its fantastic barbeque cuisine and vibrant musical history, was just itching for a professional sports team. The city had already proven that it was full of eager hoops fans by the popularity of their college basketball team, the Memphis Tigers. They even had a stunning arena—the Great American Pyramid Arena (commonly called the Pyramid Arena), that overlooked the Mississippi River. This arena was actually shaped like a giant pyramid, and brought to mind great empires,

A Walk Through History

Memphis is no longer the capital city of Egypt. Cairo has had that honor since 1168 AD.

Time for a Change

Though Memphis initially thought that the Pyramid Arena was NBA ready, they built a new basketball arena after it became clear that the Pyramid was outdated, and prone to accidents like flooding. The Grizzlies now play in FedExForum.

and pharaohs ruling beside the Nile River in Egypt. Memphis, after all, was named after the ancient capital city of Egypt.

When the Grizzlies moved to Memphis, the team decided to keep its name. Not only was it a financial hassle to re-brand a franchise, but who wouldn't want to be represented by one of the largest, toughest, and most noble animals in the entire world? So, the Grizzlies moved south to Tennessee at the end of the 2000-01 season, bringing with them their fierce name and

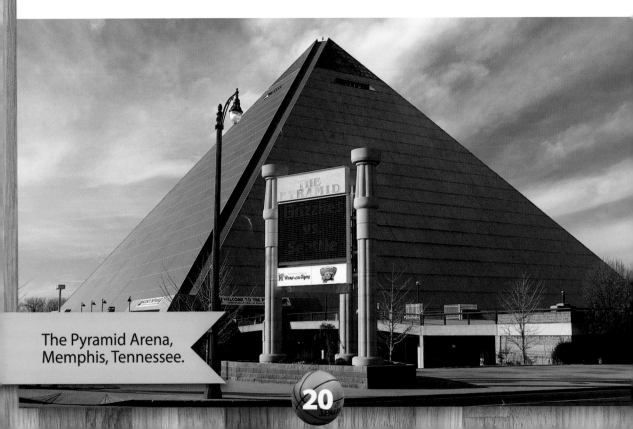

The Pyramid Arena, Memphis, Tennessee.

intimidating logo—an angry grizzly clutching a basketball in one paw, and swiping the air with the other.

However, the team itself, with its 25-57 regular season record, needed to make some serious changes before it would frighten the rest of the NBA. The Grizzlies' management decided to shake up the roster in a huge way. In the spring of 2001, Memphis sent away the face of their franchise to the Atlanta Hawks. They traded Atlanta the 27th overall pick in the 2001 draft, and Shareef Abdur-Rahim, for two veteran players and a tall rookie named Pau Gasol. Fans didn't know it yet, but—like Michael Jordan and the Chicago Bulls, or John Stockton and the Utah Jazz—the last name "Gasol" would become forever paired with the Memphis Grizzlies.

Pau Gasol proudly dons his Memphis jersey.

Chapter 3
Pow!

Unlike many NBA players, Pau Gasol did not grow up in the United States. He was actually born and raised in Barcelona, Spain—making him one of the growing number of foreign talent in the NBA. Pau's parents, who both worked in the medical industry, named him after the hospital where he was born—Sant Pau Hospital. Medicine had such a strong influence on young Pau's life, Pau even studied in the medical field for a year before he left to pursue a professional basketball career. This made a lot of sense, looking back, because Pau Gasol was just the medicine that the ailing Grizzlies needed.

When the 7' Pau Gasol joined the Grizzlies for the 2001-02 season, many people all around the world were already familiar with this young player. Before entering the NBA draft in 2001, Pau had helped Barcelona win the Spanish National Cup, where he was named Most Valuable Player. Though he was highly successful in his native Spain, Pau Gasol wanted

Before he was a star in the NBA, Pau Gasol played basketball in Spain.

Pau Gasol poses during the NBA Draft. He was first drafted by the Hawks, then traded to the Grizzlies.

Pau Gasol and the Grizzlies were each starting a brand new chapter in the NBA.

During his first season with the Memphis Grizzlies, Pau stood out in many ways. Not only was he tall, foreign, with a cool name that sounded like a comic book sound effect (pronounced Pow!), but he played like a phenom. As a power forward / center, Pau Gasol started out strong—he averaged 17.6 points per game, and ranked first among NBA rookies for blocks and rebounds. It was no surprise when Gasol captured the 2002 NBA Rookie of the Year award—making Gasol the first Grizz to ever take home the postseason's top rookie honor. Memphis still

to try his luck in the NBA. After he was chosen third overall in the 2001 NBA Draft by the Atlanta Hawks, he was immediately traded to the Vancouver Grizzlies—just as the team was transitioning to Memphis.

Pow!

Some of Pau Gasol's nicknames include "Pow!", "Power Gasol", "Kung Pow" and "The Meal Ticket."

posted a losing record for the 2001-02 season, but Pau Gasol brought hope for the future of the young team.

Several other talented players joined the Grizzlies during their first year in Memphis. One of the more well-known players at the time was Jason Williams. Williams already had a few NBA seasons under his belt when he was traded to the Grizzlies. Famous for his enthusiasm on the court, Williams was well-received in Memphis. He played with a flair, and was very exciting to watch—using behind-the-back, and no-look passes. As a rookie with the Sacramento Kings, Williams' jersey (number 55)

was the 5th highest selling jersey in the NBA. When he joined Pau Gasol in Memphis for the 2001-02 season, Williams was a ready-made star, and became one of the faces of the rebuilding franchise.

Another promising new addition to the Grizzlies' roster was Shane Battier, who came to Memphis as

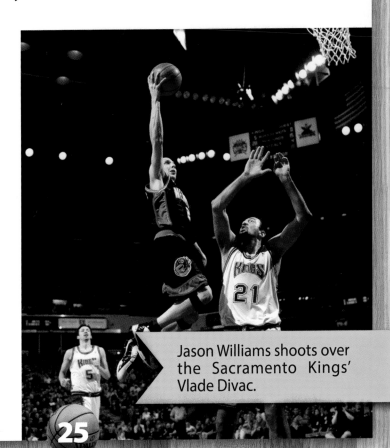

Jason Williams shoots over the Sacramento Kings' Vlade Divac.

Shane Battier won the Got Milk? Rookie of the Month Award for December 2001.

the 6th overall pick in the 2001 NBA Draft. Unlike Pau Gasol, Battier was chosen by the Grizzlies, rather than being picked by another team and then traded. At 6'8", Battier was not quite as imposing of a figure as the seven-foot Gasol, but he entered the NBA with an impressive list of college honors. After leading the Duke Blue Devils to the Final Four twice, Battier was awarded the National Player of the Year award in 2001, and had his number 31 jersey retired by Duke.

Gasol, Battier, and Williams formed a solid defensive backbone for Memphis, and they were also the top three scorers on the roster. However, the 2001-02 Grizzlies team was still not a competitive force in the NBA. Memphis needed more than talent on the court—they needed a leader.

In 2002, Coach Hubie Brown had been retired from coaching for 15 years, and was working as a TV analyst. Brown had left behind a legacy of coaching greatness, and wasn't afraid to take on a struggling team. In 1977-78, Brown won Coach of the Year after improving the Atlanta Hawks' record from 31-51 to 41-41. When the Grizzlies' GM, Jerry West, called Brown in November of 2002 and asked him to take over as head coach in Memphis, Brown didn't hesitate. At age 69, Brown would be the oldest coach in the league, but he was ready for another shot at a more active role in the NBA.

When Coach Brown arrived in Memphis, two weeks into the 2002-03 season, the Grizzlies had a dreadful 0-8 record. Hubie Brown immediately went to work on elevating the Grizzlies to a competitive level.

He focused on both their physical and mental strength. Brown later said that he wasn't afraid that Memphis couldn't win, but that they didn't *believe* that they could: "We [the coaches] stayed positive

Coach Hubie Brown during his award-winning 1977-78 season with the Atlanta Hawks.

27

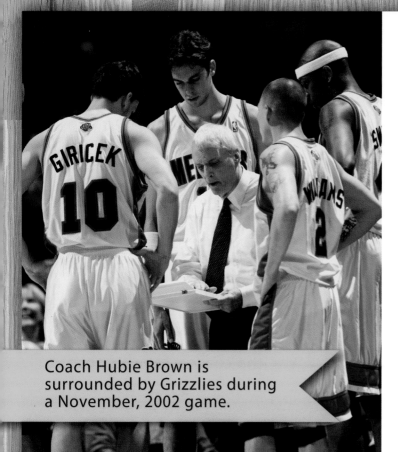

Coach Hubie Brown is surrounded by Grizzlies during a November, 2002 game.

but things were definitely changing for the better. Though they got off to a very rocky start, by the middle of the season they notched separate four- and six-game winning streaks that had the city of Memphis believing in its home team. However, Coach Brown's changes really began to pay off during the following season. The Grizzlies posted an impressive 50-32 record in 2003-04. Not only was this the Grizzlies' first winning season, but they also advanced to the playoffs for the first time in franchise history.

in everything we did. I wanted the players to understand why the team was losing, what changes we had to make and what we needed to do to win. I didn't want them to feel satisfied in coming close."

The Grizzlies closed out the 2002-03 season with a 32-50 record,

Though they didn't advance past the first round, it was still an

Pau Gasol battles the Spurs during the 2004 playoffs.

amazing turnaround for Memphis. People across the country were taking notice of the Grizzlies as potential postseason threats. After organizing this remarkable change, Coach Hubie Brown was awarded the 2004 Coach of the Year Award— his second such award in 26 years.

Grizzlies fans were thrilled with their exciting roster, award-winning coach, and fantastic regular season record. It felt like the Grizzlies had just woken up from a decade-long hibernation, and they couldn't wait to see what the next few seasons would bring.

Coach for the Ages
The 26 years between Coach Hubie Brown's first and second Coach of the Year awards was the longest such span in NBA History.

Chapter 4
TRADING PLACES

For the next two years, it was great to be a Memphis Grizzlies fan. From 2004 to 2006, there was an air of hope surrounding the growing franchise as the Grizzlies became postseason regulars. Though Memphis often exited in the first round, many fans hoped that soon—with their stellar roster, and excellent leadership on and off the court—they would start advancing further and further in the playoffs.

In 2005, Coach Hubie Brown, who had set the Grizzlies on the right path, retired from coaching due to health problems. Given Coach Brown's age—he was 71 when he officially retired— this news didn't come as a complete surprise to Grizzlies fans. Luckily, Coach Brown had instilled a winning spirit in his team, and a dedicated workout regime. Memphis still made the 2006 playoffs, and posted their second best regular season record: 49-33. It seemed like the Grizzlies were still a team on the rise.

Pau Gasol, the Grizzlies' star,

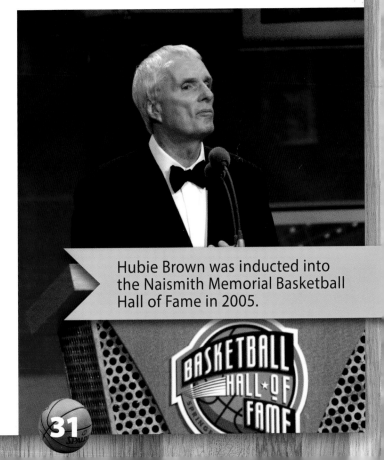

Hubie Brown was inducted into the Naismith Memorial Basketball Hall of Fame in 2005.

New Home Town

Pau Gasol's family lived in Tennessee while their son played for the Grizzlies. His brother, Marc Gasol, even went to high school in Memphis.

continued to prove his worth on the court. He was selected for the 2006 All-Star team—becoming not only the first Grizz to receive that honor, but the first player from Spain to become an All-Star. Gasol also became the Grizzlies' all-time leading rebounder during the 2005-06 season.

Then, disaster struck. In September, 2006, Pau Gasol briefly returned to Spain to compete in the International Basketball Federation world championships. This should have been a joyful time for Pau—an opportunity to play for the country that he was proud to call home.

Unfortunately, during one of

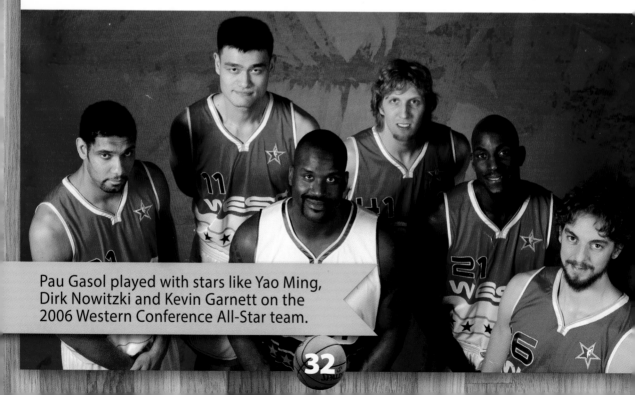

Pau Gasol played with stars like Yao Ming, Dirk Nowitzki and Kevin Garnett on the 2006 Western Conference All-Star team.

the games, Pau broke a bone in his left foot. While he healed, Pau was forced to sit out the first 23 games in the 2006-07 NBA season. The Grizzlies didn't fare well without their star, and did not recover in time to reach the playoffs—ending their three-year postseason streak.

Injured Pau Gasol is carried off the court by his brother Marc, and another teammate, during the 2006 World Basketball Championship.

Memphis realized that having one great player like Gasol was not enough to turn their team into future champions, or even consistent playoff contenders. For all of Pau Gasol's talent, the team had yet to actually win a game in the postseason. They needed a grouping of solid players, who could eventually make up a strong, consistent roster. In the middle of the 2007-08 season, the Grizzlies made a decision that rocked the franchise to its core: they traded Pau Gasol to the Los Angeles Lakers.

Memphis sent Pau Gasol to L.A.

Marc and Pau show off their silver medals after playing for Spain during the 2008 Olympics.

in exchange for four players and two future first round NBA Draft picks. One of the four players just so happened to be Marc Gasol, Pau's younger brother. This was the first time in history that an NBA team had traded one brother for another. Many people thought that Memphis had made a huge mistake. Some fans even wanted the NBA to veto a trade that appeared to be so lop-sided. It looked like the Grizzlies had just given away their star for a lesser version. Marc Gasol, who was almost five years younger than his brother Pau, was drafted by the Lakers in 2007. But he did not actually take the court until he arrived in Memphis in 2008. This new Gasol was untested in the NBA, and Grizzlies fans were worried that he would only be a shadow of his older brother.

Soon, Marc Gasol showed Memphis that he was not the "lesser" brother. During his rookie season, Marc broke the franchise rookie record for highest field goal percentage. And the player whose record Marc broke? His brother Pau's. Then, during the 2010-11 season, Gasol helped make team history. For the first time ever, the Grizzlies advanced to the Western Conference Semifinals. This was also the first season that they had ever won a game in the postseason. They beat the San Antonio Spurs, 4-2, and then forced the Oklahoma City Thunder to a seven-game series.

Several other players formed this amazing 2010-11 Grizzlies team. Power forward Zach Randolph, who was nicknamed "Z-Bo," was the team's leading scorer. Since he began his NBA career in 2001, Randolph

Marc Gasol grabs the rebound during a 2008 game against the Orlando Magic.

Z-Bo

Zach Randolph got his nickname as a child, when a friend started calling him "Z-Bo" after the character "Deebo" from the 1995 movie *Friday*.

had played for the Portland Trail Blazers, New York Knicks, and the L.A. Clippers, before joining the Grizzlies in 2009. Once in Memphis, Randolph's game began to seriously take off. In 2010, Randolph was selected for his first All-Star game. It was no surprise when, in 2011, he helped lead the Grizzlies to the playoffs for the first time in four years.

Forward Rudy Gay, who had started his NBA career with the Grizzlies in 2006, had become the new team leader after Pau Gasol's departure in 2008. Though Rudy helped the Grizzlies during their big 2010-11 season return to prominence, he unfortunately had a season-ending shoulder injury, and was forced to sit out the entire postseason. Guards Mike Conley and O.J. Mayo were also key players

Z-Bo celebrates after the Grizzlies advance to the 2011 Western Conference Semifinals.

Rudy Gay dunks against Jeff Green of the Oklahoma City Thunder during a 2011 game.

on the Grizzlies' journey back to the playoffs. This new momentum continued through 2012, when the Grizzlies advanced to the postseason for the fifth time in team history. It looked like the things were finally back on track for Memphis.

In October of 2012, another big change shook up Memphis. The Grizzlies franchise was bought by an ownership group headed by billionaire Robert Pera. At 34 years old, Pera was the youngest person to ever own an NBA team. Pera made his living by being on the cutting edge of technology. His company, Ubiquiti Networks, created hardware that revolutionized the wireless internet world.

After buying the Grizzlies, Pera wanted his team to be cutting edge too. The NBA had just started

Robert Pera and Jason Levien: the new owner, and CEO, respectively, of the Memphis Grizzlies.

for any new innovation, hired new CEO Jason Levien, who subsequently hired John Hollinger as the new vice president of basketball operations. Hollinger was famous for his stats-oriented basketball columns for ESPN—he created the Player Efficiency Rating (PER), and was one of the greatest statistical minds in the NBA.

With Hollinger in Memphis, the Grizzlies had a huge leg up in the growing statistical analysis field. In fact, this new attention to stats influenced some major roster moves in early 2013—including a complicated, six-player, three-team trade that sent star Rudy Gay to the Toronto Raptors. In exchange, the

to embrace advanced statistical analysis—a practice that was commonplace in Major League Baseball, but was just starting to become mainstream for the NBA. Pera, who was always first in line

Wireless Wonder

Robert Pera earned the nickname "Wireless Wonder," when his goal of bringing affordable wireless technology to the masses made him a billionaire.

Grizzlies acquired several players, among them former Detroit Piston Tayshaun Prince—a small forward who had helped Detroit win the NBA Championship in 2004.

All of those changes made the city of Memphis wary, but hopeful. And fans were about to see if new owner Robert Pera's strategies would pay off, as the Grizzlies took on the OKC Thunder in the 2013 Western Conference Semifinals.

Coming Home
One of the other members of the Memphis Grizzlies ownership group is actor/singer Justin Timberlake. This star was born in Memphis.

Tayshaun Prince, Marc Gasol, Tony Allen, Mike Conley, and Zach Randolph convene during the 2013 postseason.

WE DON'T
BLUFF.

2013 NBA Playoffs | GRIZZLIES SPURS

GRIZZLIES
50

BLUFF

When the Memphis Grizzlies and the OKC Thunder went head-to-head in the 2013 Western Conference Semifinals, many NBA fans thought they knew how the series would end—with the Thunder on top. After all, they had seen it all before in 2011, when the Grizzlies and Thunder battled it out in seven grueling games during the 2011 Western Conference Semifinals. During their previous match-up, the Grizzlies and Thunder traded victories, until the Thunder—led by young superstars Kevin Durant and Russell Westbrook—put the final nail in the series' coffin with a crushing Game 7 victory in Oklahoma City.

So, when the Grizzlies lost Game 1 of the 2013 Western Conference Semifinals to the Thunder, it seemed a little too familiar. Most of

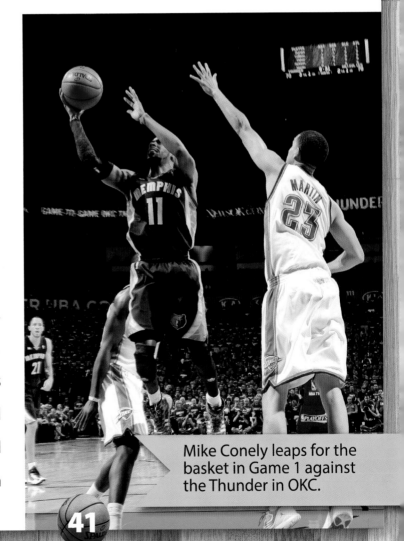

Mike Conely leaps for the basket in Game 1 against the Thunder in OKC.

Theme Song

A pair of locally born rappers—Drumma Boy and DJ Paul—wrote a theme song for the Grizzlies titled, "We Don't Bluff." This slogan is also a play on Memphis' nickname—the Bluff City—named because Memphis sits on the bluffs overlooking the Mississippi River.

the country thought the Grizzlies might put up a good fight, only to fall short again. "Just wait," Memphis fans would say to doubters. "Just wait until the Thunder enter the 'Grindhouse.'"

The Grizzlies had adopted a new slogan for the 2012-13 season, to go along with their "Grit-&-Grind" style of play: "We Don't Bluff." This slogan was coined by Zach Randolph during an early 2012-13 game against the Thunder, when he said of his straightforward, determined playing style: "I don't bluff." Sports writer Eric Freeman sums up what these words meant to the Grizzlies: "This team doesn't back down to challenges, attempts to enforce their style upon the game at any cost, and simply won't quit

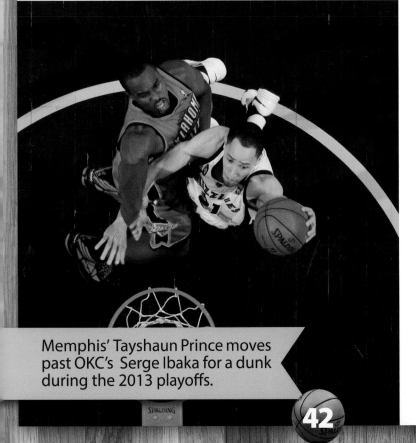

Memphis' Tayshaun Prince moves past OKC's Serge Ibaka for a dunk during the 2013 playoffs.

until the rules of the sport dictate they must leave the court. They mean what they say, and we know this because their actions do most of their talking for them."

Much to Tennessee's delight, the Grizzlies went on to steal Game 2 from the Thunder in OKC's Chesapeake Energy Arena. They returned home to Memphis with the series all tied up. When Grizzlies fans packed the stands for Game 3, they waved promotional yellow towels that said "We Don't Bluff," "Believe," or "Grit, Grind" in big, blue letters. As Marc Gasol and Zach Randolph took the court, they weren't

Memphis fans show that they "believe" in their team during Game 3 of the Western Conference Semifinals.

bluffing about how confident they felt, and how much they wanted a victory that night. If they kept up the momentum and won the series, Memphis would advance to the Western Conference Finals for the first time in franchise history. Putting the Thunder in a 2-1 hole

OKC's Kevin Durant tries to drive past Zach Randolph in the 2013 playoffs.

key player from the 2012-13 regular season. Guard Russell Westbrook, who was Kevin Durant's other half on the court, had torn cartilage in his leg early in the first round of the playoffs. OKC fans were devastated by this loss, but they were also confident that the remaining stars on their team would make quick work of the Grizzlies—even in the "Grindhouse."

would go a long way towards accomplishing that feat.

Though the Thunder had a tough roster, they were missing one

Believe!
Many Grizzlies fans held up yellow towels that read "Believe Memphis." This slogan also was first used in the 2011 playoff series against the Thunder.

Game 3 was a hard-fought duel from the very beginning, with each teams' defense keeping the score close. Kevin Durant, however, made his mark on the game in the first two quarters—posting 16 points, and keeping his team tight with the

Grizzlies. At halftime, the Thunder were ahead 45-44. But the third quarter belonged to Memphis. Marc Gasol not only showed off his award-winning defensive skills, but he scored 15 points in the third quarter alone. The "Grindhouse" erupted with cheers every time Gasol sank a shot or made a free throw, and yellow towels waved like victory banners. At the end of the third quarter, the score was 66-60, Memphis.

The Thunder tried to recover in the fourth quarter. They even managed to tie up the game with two minutes to go. Though Memphis fans hated to see the score so tight, they still believed in the power of the Grizzlies' home court. During the final two minutes of the game, Marc Gasol and Mike Conley made every single free throw that

Marc Gasol was on fire against the OKC Thunder in Game 3.

Brotherly Love

Pau Gasol returned to Memphis to watch his brother play in the 2013 Western Conference Finals.

they attempted—sinking all six shots. The Thunder, on the other hand, simply crumbled. They missed everything they threw at the rim. When the final second ticked away, the Grizzlies were victorious—87-81.

The Grizzlies went on to win the next two games against the Thunder, nearly sweeping the series, 4-1. Their final win was on OKC's home court—the same court where the Grizzlies had been bested in the Western Conference Semifinals just two years earlier. Though Memphis was not able to defeat the Spurs in the Western Conference Finals, the Grizzlies had shown the world a whole new level of excellence and determination. All eyes

Kevin Durant congratulates Marc Gasol after the Grizzlies' Western Conference Semifinals victory.

Coach David Joerger and Tony Allen run defensive drills.

will be on the young team from Memphis, as the league waits to see what the next many seasons will bring.

Memphis management worked hard to keep the Grizzlies' core group together—re-signing Tony Allen, and keeping other key players like Gasol and Randolph home in Tennessee rather than making any huge roster changes. They also added a new head coach to the mix in the form of longtime Grizzlies assistant coach David Joerger, after parting ways with Lionel Hollins. Joerger had emerged as one of

Bobble-Coach?
While David Joerger was coaching for the D-League Dakota Wizards, the team made a bobble-head figurine of Joerger, which was passed out to the first 400 fans at a game.

the most successful coaches in the minor leagues of basketball—earning five championships during his time with the International Basketball Association (IBA), Continental Basketball Association (CBA), and the NBA's D-League. As the Grizzlies' assistant coach for six years, Joerger was also instrumental in helping Memphis reach their—now famous—Grit-&-Grind level of defense.

The Grizzlies' tough-as-nails roster, and new leadership off the court, filled Memphis fans with hope for the future. With their city's overwhelming support behind them, there is no limit to what Memphis can accomplish in the coming years. Perhaps, very soon, the Grizzlies will claw their way to the NBA's pinnacle, and finally hang a Championship banner in the "Grindhouse."

The Grizzlies' 2013 Western Conference Finals appearance marked their best season in franchise history.